1. Introduction

One of the more interesting facets of voluntary exchange is how changes in the strategic environment lead to differences in transaction outcomes. For example, increasing the value of a player's threat-point payoff increases their payoff from Nash bargaining. The theoretical work in Holt [1980] shows that switching from first-price auction rules to second-price auction rules decreases the auctioneer's expected payoff if bidders are risk averse. Finally, comparing the pioneering experimental work in Chamberlin [1948] and Smith [1962] illustrates that changing the nature of the information available to the players can dramatically influence the price and efficiency of an exchange process. With this insight in mind, in this paper we use the experimental method to examine and compare four exchange mechanisms in a procurement setting in which a buyer faces several sellers that have privately known production costs.

The first two institutions are variants of the multilateral negotiations introduced in Thomas and Wilson [2001]. In this common exchange mechanism, a buyer solicits price offers from multiple sellers, and then it elicits more favorable offers by playing the sellers off one another until it accepts one of the offers or breaks off the negotiations. Among other settings, multilateral negotiations are pervasive in industrial procurement, the securing of high-end job offers, and the purchasing of expensive goods such as computers, contractors' services, and automobiles.

The second two institutions are the first-price auction and the second-price auction. These well-known auction formats and their theoretically isomorphic variants, the Dutch auction and the English auction, are used extensively to allocate products as varied as flowers, art, produce, fish, government securities, and offshore mineral rights.[1] More recently, several governments have used auctions to allocate such valuable resources as radio spectra, electric power, and pollution rights.[2]

We hypothesize that the outcome of a multilateral negotiation is critically influenced by the buyer's ability to credibly reveal to a seller the price offers it holds from other sellers. With that hypothesis in mind, in Thomas and Wilson [2001] we investigated *nonverifiable multilateral negotiations*, in which the buyer cannot credibly reveal the best offer it currently holds. In many negotiation settings it is reasonable to assume that the buyer is unable or unwilling to credibly

---

[1] See Milgrom and Weber [1982] and McAfee and McMillan [1987].
[2] See McAfee and McMillan [1996], Wolfram [1998], and Cason [1995] for details, respectively.

reveal rival sellers' offers. We compared nonverifiable negotiations to first-price auctions, because the two institutions appeared to be conceptually similar. We found that the two institutions' prices are indistinguishable with four sellers, but that negotiated prices exceed auction prices with two sellers.

In this paper we investigate *verifiable multilateral negotiations*, in which the buyer can credibly reveal the best offer it currently holds. Internet-based third-party business-to-business exchanges provide one of the best examples of institutions in which a buyer could credibly reveal its best offer. As an independent third party with a reputation to maintain and legal responsibilities to uphold, a business-to-business exchange can credibly authenticate the best offer that a buyer currently holds. Even though most people likely view auctions as the dominant exchange mechanism in B2B commerce, negotiations are becoming more common on B2B sites. For example, at www.chemconnect.com, a purchasing manager can invite its suppliers into a "Corporate Trading Room" to settle on a transaction for raw chemical materials.[3] We compare verifiable negotiations to second-price auctions because, as we will argue, the two institutions appear to be conceptually similar. Moreover, examining these two institutions naturally complements our earlier work.

In addition to comparing the outcomes of verifiable multilateral negotiations and second-price auctions, we integrate those results with the results of our earlier experiment that compared nonverifiable multilateral negotiations and first-price auctions. The integrated results provide a detailed picture of the relationships among the four institutions.

The outcomes of multilateral negotiations are not only interesting in their own right. Their relationship to the outcomes of various auction formats is interesting because of its implications for institutional design. The fact that some buyers in an industry use multilateral negotiations, while others use one-shot sealed-bid auctions, suggests either that the processes are outcome-equivalent or that there are factors that make one process more favorable than the other. Identifying these factors should lead to a more informed selection of an exchange process.

We study the relationship between second-price auctions and verifiable multilateral negotiations by permitting fairly unstructured negotiation between a buyer and several sellers. Each experimental session anonymously matches a buyer with either two or four sellers, and

---

[3] The World Chemical Exchange at www.chemconnect.com reports that it in first quarter of 2001, more than $2 billion worth of transactions were conducted at its site.

consists of several periods of negotiations and second-price auctions. When multilateral negotiations are employed, the buyer can communicate electronically in real-time with the sellers, but the sellers cannot communicate with each other. When auctions are employed, the buyer plays a passive role, and none of the players can communicate with each other. We match sellers' costs across sessions and institutions to study whether outcomes depend on which institution is used. Similarly, we vary the number of sellers to see how the outcomes change within an institution.

We find that transaction prices are strictly lower in verifiable multilateral negotiations than in second-price auctions, despite the two institutions' seeming equivalence. Price-setting in the second-price auctions largely reflects the sellers' dominant strategy, and the across-institution price difference emerges when there is a large spread between the lowest and second-lowest costs. In those cases the low-cost seller's initial offer in the negotiations tends to be below the second-lowest cost, eliminating the need for further negotiation. When the cost spread is small, the two institutions' prices are statistically indistinguishable and are approximately equal to the second-lowest cost. Using the results of our earlier study, we also compare the two institutions with first-price auctions and with nonverifiable multilateral negotiations. All four institutions are highly efficient, with second-price auctions yielding the highest prices, followed in order by verifiable negotiations, nonverifiable negotiations, and first-price auctions.

The paper is structured as follows. Section 2 describes the framework we envision underlying both the auction and the negotiation settings, and it explains the reasoning behind our hypothesis that the outcomes of second-price auctions and multilateral negotiations should be identical. Section 3 describes the experimental design and the procedures we use to examine the relationship between the two institutions. Sections 4 and 5 present our within-experiment and across-experiment results, respectively, while Section 6 briefly concludes.

2. Related Theoretical Background

While auctions have been studied extensively, multilateral negotiations have not been formally modeled in the bargaining literature, presumably due to their strategic complexity. Hence, our study is based upon our intuition about how second-price auctions and verifiable multilateral negotiations should be related. We explain that intuition below, but first we describe second-price auction theory and our conception of how verifiable multilateral negotiations are executed.

Consider a setting in which T risk-neutral sellers compete to fulfill a contract for a single risk-neutral buyer. V_B is the commonly known value that the buyer places on having the contract fulfilled. Each seller's cost c is a privately known independent draw from the continuous distribution function G with density g that is strictly positive over the support $[\underline{c},\overline{c}]$. In the auction literature, this is referred to as a symmetric independent private value (IPV) setting.

The second-price auction proceeds with each seller simultaneously submitting a secret price offer. The seller offering the lowest price is awarded the contract at the lesser of the next highest price offered and V_B, provided the lowest price is less than V_B. All other sellers receive nothing. The winning seller's profit is $p - c_w$, where p is the transaction price and c_w is the winning seller's cost. The buyer's profit is $V_B - p$, total surplus is $V_B - c_w$, and efficiency is $(V_B - c_w)/(V_B - c_1)$, where c_1 is the lowest realized cost. Each seller's unique dominant strategy is to offer a price equal to its cost.

The multilateral negotiation proceeds with each seller simultaneously making a secret price offer to the buyer in the first period of play. The buyer can accept one of the offers or reject them all. If the buyer accepts an offer, then the game concludes and the transaction price is the price p offered by the winning seller. As in the auction setting, the winning seller's profit is $p - c_w$, where c_w is the winning seller's cost, and the buyer's profit is $V_B - p$. If the buyer rejects all offers, then the buyer simultaneously announces to each seller the best standing offer it possesses.[4] The sellers can respond to this communication by making additional price offers, the buyer can accept or reject these new offers, and so on. The game continues in this fashion until a transaction occurs.

Within the auction literature, it has been hypothesized that multilateral negotiations bear some relation to second-price or English auctions (e.g., see Waehrer and Perry [1999]). The general argument is that the buyer should be able to obtain concessions from a seller until the seller's offer is just equal to the seller's cost, with the implicit assumption that the negotiations conclude when only a single seller remains. We agree in part with this conjecture, but our intuition is that the relationship between multilateral negotiations and various auction formats

---

[4] As an alternative formulation, one could consider a setting in which the buyer can credibly reveal rivals' offers, but must inform the sellers individually rather than simultaneously.

depends critically on the buyer's ability to credibly reveal to a seller its rivals' offers. Specifically, if the offers can be credibly revealed, then the multilateral negotiation should be similar to a second-price or English auction, because sellers should be willing to make concessions until the price reaches their cost. If the offers cannot be credibly revealed, then the multilateral negotiation should be similar to a first-price auction.

To understand why the ability to credibly reveal offers might play a crucial role, consider the problem facing a seller in a multilateral negotiation when its rivals' offers cannot be credibly revealed. When the buyer tries to use a rival's offer to elicit a better offer from the seller, the seller must be concerned that the buyer is not being truthful about the terms or the existence of the rival's offer. Consequently, the seller must be aware of the danger that he could end up bidding against himself by offering price reductions that are undercut by fictitious discounts from a rival. This danger is not present when the best offer can be credibly revealed.

For several reasons, the preceding relationships may not be exact, either empirically or theoretically. First, in practice the outcomes of multilateral negotiations likely depend critically on the players' ability to haggle. For example, once the buyer determines which seller has the lowest cost in a verifiable multilateral negotiation, the buyer and that seller still may negotiate over the division of the remaining surplus. To the extent that the buyer is able to extract further concessions from the low-cost seller once the price has reached the second-lowest cost, then the negotiated price will be lower than the price in the second-price auction.

Second, in multilateral negotiations there must be incentives for sellers to make serious offers. That is, there is no reason for sellers to make an offer until the last possible moment, particularly if there are no delay costs[5] and if they are concerned that serious initial offers either will be used against them by the buyer later in the negotiation, or will provoke a sequence of aggressive price cuts.[6] This effect would tend to make negotiated prices exceed second-price auction prices. In our experimental framework, there exists a time limit on each negotiation period, and there clearly exist frictions that prevent the buyer from receiving infinitely many offers. Consequently, there are delay costs, and a seller might be concerned that it will be left

---

[5] Regardless of the verifiability of offers, a multilateral negotiation will be equivalent to a first-price auction if the buyer's cost of obtaining additional offers exceeds the maximum possible gain from obtaining those offers, or if the discount factor is zero (so that future transactions have no value). In both cases the buyer will accept one of the initial offers.

[6] Roth and Ockenfels [2001] provide evidence to suggest that concerns of this nature lead to last-minute bidding, or "sniping," in online auctions with a fixed ending time.

out of the communication process if it does not make serious offers. These market frictions would tend to reduce negotiated prices, but not necessarily to a level below that of second-price auction prices.

3. Experimental Design and Procedures

Using "S" to denote a sequence of second-price auctions and "V" to denote a sequence of verifiable multilateral negotiations, we pair two treatments, one with the sequence $VSSV$, and one with the sequence $SSVS$. The first and third sequences consist of 12 transactions; the second consists of 16, while the fourth consists of 6.[7] Later we refer to each of the four sequences as a "regime." We vary these two treatments by changing the number of sellers. One has two sellers per buyer, while the other has four sellers per buyer.

For each of the four treatments, {2 sellers, 4 sellers} × {$VSSV$, $SSVS$}, we have four groups of subjects. Each subject is assigned a specific role in a specific group for the duration of the experiment. A seller's characteristics consist of 46 random cost draws from the Uniform distribution on the support [0.00, 6.00], one for each time period. Of the eight groups with four sellers, seller i (i = 1, 2, 3, 4) has the same cost draws across groups. Of the eight groups with two sellers, seller i (i = 1, 2) has the same cost draws across groups. Moreover, the costs of sellers 1 and 2 in the two-seller treatment are the same as the costs of sellers 1 and 2 in the four-seller treatment.

Our experiment consisted of a total of 736 second-price auctions or rounds of verifiable multilateral negotiations using 64 undergraduate student volunteers (48 sellers and 16 buyers). Some students had participated previously in market experiments, but with substantially different trading institutions. No subject participated in more than one of the sessions.

In addition to reading self-paced instructions displayed by the software, the subjects followed along as the experiment monitor read aloud from a handout with both additional and review information.[8] The public instructions explained (and made common knowledge) that the sellers' costs were assigned randomly each period and that the distribution of the draws was

---
[7] We employ these sequences, rather than the more common SVS and VSV sequences of treatments, to permit comparisons with the experimental results regarding first-price auctions and nonverifiable multilateral negotiations in Thomas and Wilson [2001]. The experiment reported in that paper used such sequences to get a sufficient number of auction observations while satisfying a time constraint on the experiment's length.

$U[0.00, 6.00]$. The instructions also revealed that the buyer's value was 6.00. Revealing the buyer's value is consistent with prior buying auction experiments in which bids are constrained to be nonnegative, which effectively bounds the buyers' bids between zero and their respective values. Here, we effectively bound the sellers' price offers between their respective costs and 6.00.

The random cost draw for a given period was disclosed to the subject at the beginning of the period. In the second-price auction environment, after learning his cost each seller had four minutes to submit his private offer to sell, though this limit was never binding. The computer automatically awarded the sale to the seller that submitted the lowest offer once all of the offers had been submitted, provided that the lowest offer was less than 6.00. The winning seller was paid the lower of the second-lowest price and the buyer's value. At the end of the auction, the final market price was announced electronically to all market participants, after which the session proceeded to the next period.

In the verifiable multilateral negotiation environment, after learning his cost each seller had 30 seconds in the first phase of the period to submit his initial offer to the buyer. The instructions indicated that the seller would be able to lower his offer at any time in the second phase of the period by submitting a new binding offer. Once the buyer received all initial offers, the clock was reset to four minutes for the negotiation phase. At any time during the negotiation phase, a seller could (only) lower his offer, and the buyer could accept the offer of a single seller. Furthermore, a buyer and a specific seller could use text messaging over the computer network to engage in nonbinding discussions concerning a transaction. The buyer could negotiate individually with any seller, but only one at a time, while retaining standing offers from the other sellers. In contrast, sellers could only communicate with their buyer. A transcript of the discussions between the buyer and the seller remained on the screen for the duration of the period. The subjects only knew the laboratory identification number of the parties with whom they were communicating. Once the buyer accepted an offer, the final market price was announced electronically to all market participants,[9] after which the session proceeded to the

---

[8] The instructions for the second-price auctions are based upon those used by Cox, Roberson, and Smith [1982] and Cox, Smith, and Walker [1983, 1988]. The instructions for the multilateral negotiations are newly developed, but follow those for the second-price auctions to the extent possible.

[9] There were only two cases in which the buyer did not accept any offer. Both of these were in the two-seller treatment when the costs of *both* sellers were relatively close to 6.00.

next period. At all times, the best submitted offer was visible to all participants, and they all were informed in the instructions that this was the case.

The subjects were not told the number of trading periods in the session or in any institutional regime within the session. Moreover, the subjects did not know the nature of any future trading institution, as the instructions for an institution were displayed only prior to commencing trade. It was public information that the same set of sellers was matched with the same buyer for the duration of the experiment. Such repeated play is a common feature of naturally occurring markets and previous auction experiments.[10]

Participants received $5 for showing up on time, plus their salient earnings. In the four-seller sessions, the buyers' exchange rate was US$1 for 7 experimental dollars, and the sellers' exchange rate was US$1.50 for 1 experimental dollar. In the two-seller sessions, the exchange amounts were 4 and 2 experimental dollars for each US$1, respectively. To equalize the buyers' and sellers' earnings expectations, the exchange rates are more favorable to the sellers because a buyer receives a payoff every period, but a seller only expects to win every two or four periods. Based upon the theoretical second-price auction outcomes for the observed cost draws, these exchange rates reflect an average cash payoff of $21.50 for all types of agents. In addition to the $5 fee for showing up on time, the average subject's earnings for this experiment were $20.50. The average session lasted 75 to 90 minutes.

4. Within-Experiment Results

For each period of play, our data set includes the transaction price, each seller's cost, each seller's initial and subsequent offers in the multilateral negotiations, and a verbatim record of the communications between buyers and sellers. The latter is not part of our statistical analysis, but it provides qualitative insights about the players' strategies and their beliefs about other's strategies. The data permit us to compare the transaction prices and efficiency for the different institutions and numbers of sellers, a summary of which is in Table 1.

We present our within-experiment results as a series of three findings. Our qualitative results are displayed in tables and figures, and our quantitative results are derived by analyzing

---

[10] For example, see Coppinger, Smith and Titus [1980], Cox, Roberson, and Smith [1982], Cox, Smith, and Walker [1983], and Kagel, Harstad, and Levin [1987].

the data using a linear mixed-effects model for repeated measures.[11] Table 2 reports the model's regression results for each of the four regimes. The dependent variable is the observed transaction price. The treatment effects (*Two* vs. *Four* Sellers, and *Verifiable* Negotiation vs. *Second-Price Auction*) and an interaction effect from the 2 × 2 design are modeled as (zero-one) fixed effects, while the 16 independent sessions are modeled as random effects, e_i. Specifically, we estimate the model

$$Price_{ij} = \mu + e_i + \beta_1 Two_i + \beta_2 Verifiable_i + \beta_3 Two_i \times Verifiable_i + \varepsilon_{ij},$$

where $e_i \sim N(0, \sigma_1^2)$ and $\varepsilon_{ij} \sim N(0, \sigma_{2,i}^2)$. The sessions are indexed by i and the repeated periods are indexed by j (e.g., $j = 1, 2, \ldots, 12$, for the first regime of twelve periods).[12] We accommodate heteroskedastic errors by session when estimating the model via maximum likelihood.

Estimates of the treatment effects are easy to compute with this specification. The intercept μ is the expected price in a four-seller second-price auction, $\mu + \beta_1$ is the expected price in a two-seller second-price auction, $\mu + \beta_2$ is the expected price in a four-seller verifiable multilateral negotiation, and $\mu + \beta_1 + \beta_2 + \beta_3$ is the expected price in a two-seller verifiable multilateral negotiation. Across-treatment price differences, and differences-in-differences, also are easy to compute.

Our first finding is a baseline result that establishes that the change in the number of sellers affects transaction prices in the manner predicted by standard oligopoly models.

Finding 1: *For all regimes and institutions, reducing the number of sellers from four to two significantly increases transaction prices.*

Evidence: Table 1 reports the average transaction price for the first 12 periods, by institutional regime and by the number of sellers. The average price in the second-price auctions is 3.03 with four sellers and is 4.17 with two sellers, which is a 37.6% increase. The average price in the multilateral negotiations is 2.50 with four sellers and is 3.46 with two sellers, which is a 27.7% increase. Similar price comparisons can be made for the remaining periods. The results in both institutions suggest that the transaction price increases as the number of sellers decreases.

---

[11] See Laird and Ware [1982] and Longford [1993] for a description of this technique commonly employed in experimental sciences.
[12] The linear mixed-effects model for repeated measures treats each session as one degree of freedom with respect to the treatments. Hence, with four parameters, there are 12 degrees of freedom for the estimates of the treatment fixed effects (16 sessions − 4 parameters).

Figure 1(a) displays by treatment the transaction prices in each of the first twelve periods, averaged over the four sessions in each treatment. Figures 1(b) through 1(d) display the same information for the remaining three regimes. As with the data presented in Table 1, visual examination of the average prices in the two-seller and four-seller *SSVS* treatments suggests that in each period the transaction prices are higher with fewer sellers. The same conclusion holds for the *VSSV* treatments.

The estimates in Table 2 from the linear mixed-effects model for repeated measures provide a formal test of this finding. The coefficient on the *Two* dummy variable, which measures the primary effect of the two-seller treatment, is positive and highly significant in all four regimes, raising transaction prices by $\hat{\beta}_1$ = 1.13, 1.61, 0.82, and 2.26 experimental dollars, respectively (*p*-value = 0.0013, 0.0000, 0.0191, and 0.0000). Because the coefficient $\hat{\beta}_3$ on the interaction term is insignificant in each regime, we cannot reject the null hypothesis that the price change induced by reducing the number of sellers is the same across institutions. ∎

We now turn our attention to our primary findings that compare the transaction prices and the efficiency of second-price auctions and verifiable multilateral negotiations.

Finding 2: *For all regimes with paired auctions and negotiations, verifiable multilateral negotiation prices are statistically lower than second-price auction prices with both two and four sellers. The magnitude of the across-institution price difference is invariant to the number of sellers.*

Evidence: Table 1 reports that in Regime 1, with four sellers, the average price is 3.03 in the second-price auctions and is 2.50 in the verifiable multilateral negotiations. With two sellers, the average price is 4.17 in the second-price auctions and is 3.46 in the verifiable multilateral negotiations. Price comparisons in Regimes 3 and 4 yield similar conclusions.

Reference to Figure 1, but now comparing the average prices across sequences for a fixed number of sellers, illustrates the across-institution differences per period. The price patterns in the four-seller treatments are noticeably different, as are the price patterns in the two-seller treatments.

The estimates in Table 2 provide a formal test of this finding. As we indicated earlier, the estimate of the *Verifiable* coefficient, $\hat{\beta}_2$, represents the difference between the expected prices of the multilateral negotiations and the second-price auctions, holding the number of sellers constant at four. The point estimates for Regimes 1, 3, and 4 are –0.59, –1.62, and –0.73, respectively, and are statistically significant (p-values = 0.0402, 0.0005, and 0.0276), so we reject the null hypothesis in favor of the alternative that verifiable prices are less than second-price auction prices. This is not too surprising, given our visual examination of the four-seller transaction prices in Table 1 and Figure 1. With four sellers in second-price auctions, the estimated transaction prices are given by $\hat{\mu}$, so the *Verifiable* treatment lowers four-seller transaction prices by 19%, 50%, and 27% to $\hat{\mu} + \hat{\beta}_2 =$ 2.49, 1.59, and 1.94.

For two sellers the total effect of the *Verifiable* treatment significantly lowers transaction prices in Regimes 1, 3, and 4 by $\hat{\beta}_2 + \hat{\beta}_3$ = –0.70, –1.56, and –1.40 experimental dollars, respectively, below the level for two sellers in second-price auctions (p-values = 0.0319, 0.0016, and 0.0012). Because the coefficient $\hat{\beta}_3$ on the interaction term is insignificantly different from zero, we cannot reject the null hypothesis that the across-treatment magnitudes do not change with the number of sellers. With two sellers in second-price auctions, the estimated transaction prices are given by $\hat{\mu} + \hat{\beta}_1$, so the *Verifiable* treatment lowers two-seller transaction prices by 17%, 39%, and 28% to $\hat{\mu} + \hat{\beta}_1 + \hat{\beta}_2 + \hat{\beta}_3$ = 3.50, 2.473, and 3.53. ∎

It is worth noting that verifiable negotiation prices are always lower than second-price auction prices, regardless of the sequencing of the institutions. This robustness to the ordering makes more compelling our inference from Finding 2 that the observed effects are due to the institutional treatment rather than to unidentifiable factors or sampling variation.

Despite the robustness of the price ranking of the verifiable negotiations and the second-price auctions, there is some weak evidence of a hysteresis or learning effect in Regime 2, which matches second-price auctions across the two sequence treatments. Those sessions that use verifiable multilateral negotiations in Regime 1 have somewhat higher second-price auction prices, $\hat{\beta}_2$ = 0.41 (p-value = 0.0898), as perhaps the sellers learn to play their dominant strategy. However, in Regime 3 those same sellers nearly play according to the dominant strategy for a second-price auction.

Finding 3: *For all regimes and institutions, the level of efficiency is not significantly affected by any primary or interaction effects, with one exception. There is weak evidence in Regime 1 that the primary effect of changing from auctions to multilateral negotiations slightly decreases the level of efficiency.*

Evidence: Table 1 reports the average efficiency by institutional regime and by the number of sellers. The observed high efficiency levels are consistent with those reported in previous auction experiments.[13] Table 3 reports the results from a linear mixed-effects model with the efficiency level as the dependent variable. As in our pricing analysis, the baseline treatment is four sellers in second-price auctions. In the auction treatment, reducing the number of sellers from four to two has no effect on efficiency, as the coefficient $\hat{\gamma}_1$ is insignificant for Regimes 1 through 4 (*p*-values = 0.7697, 0.3479, 0.8432 and 0.9950). The coefficient $\hat{\gamma}_3$ on the interaction term *Two* × *Verifiable* is also insignificant in all four regimes (*p*-values = 0.3702, 0.4539, 0.6764 and 0.7236). Thus, in the negotiation treatment, reducing the number of sellers from four to two has no effect on efficiency. In Regime 1 we can reject the null hypothesis at a level of 0.0764 that efficiency in the four-seller negotiations equals efficiency in the four-seller second-price auctions in favor of the alternative that efficiency in the four-seller negotiations is lower ($\hat{\gamma}_2 = -3.93$), but we fail to reject the null in Regimes 3 and 4 ($\hat{\gamma}_2 = -2.00$ and -3.64, and *p*-value = 0.5170 and 0.2923). ∎

Findings 2 and 3 report that transaction prices with both two and four sellers are strictly lower in verifiable multilateral negotiations than in second-price auctions, but that efficiency is almost always the same. From these two findings we infer that switching from verifiable multilateral negotiations to second-price auctions transfers surplus from the buyer to the most efficient seller. This suggests that the buyer should prefer employing verifiable multilateral negotiations to second-price auctions.

In Section 2 we offer possible reasons why the outcomes of auctions and negotiations might differ. Examination of the data reveals that negotiation prices are less than second-price auction prices, but not for the reasons we hypothesized *ex ante*. Figure 2 plots every period's average transaction price per treatment against that period's second-lowest cost. The second-price auction prices in red circles are highly correlated with the second-lowest cost, for both the

---

[13] cf. 10.

two-seller and four-seller treatments, which is consistent with the sellers' unique dominant strategy in the second-price auction. Moreover, a 95% prediction interval for a linear regression of the second-price auction prices on the second-lowest cost contains the 45° line, which corresponds to bidding according to the dominant strategy.[14] In marked contrast, the verifiable negotiation prices in blue diamonds are not strongly correlated with the second-lowest cost. In fact, many of the verifiable negotiation prices are *less* than the second-lowest cost and lie outside the aforementioned 95% prediction interval. Thus, while the behavior in the second-price auctions is consistent with the sellers' playing their dominant strategy, it does not reliably predict the prices in the verifiable negotiations, which are lower.

Having shown the nature of the across-treatment price difference, we can now explain why the verifiable multilateral negotiation prices are less than the second-price auction prices. Figure 3 plots the winning seller's initial offer against the second-lowest cost for each period of verifiable negotiations in all sessions. The initial offer of the winning seller (nearly always the low-cost seller, as illustrated by the efficiency results in Finding 3) is often less than the second-lowest cost. Consequently, in those instances there was no actual negotiation of prices, and the price is less than the corresponding price in the second-price auctions. In the Appendix we provide some examples from the negotiation transcripts of the sellers' offering behavior and the negotiated prices. These examples illustrate the price movement, or lack thereof, as a function of the initial offer's relationship to the second-lowest cost.

The hypothesized theoretical equivalence of second-price auctions and verifiable multilateral negotiations relies on the crucial assumption that sellers make nonserious initial offers at the buyer's value (6.00), so that offers subsequently decline. Figure 3 illustrates that this clearly is not how the sellers behave. Sellers submit initial offers at prices greater than their costs, but generally less than 6.00. One possible consequence of this behavior is that when the gap between the lowest and second-lowest cost is large, the low-cost seller's initial offer may be less than the second-lowest cost, resulting in second-price auction prices exceeding negotiated prices. When the gap between the lowest and second-lowest cost is small, the low-cost seller's initial offer is likely to exceed the second-lowest cost. In that instance, negotiated prices and

---

[14] Obviously, the sellers are not strictly bidding according to their dominant strategy, because the transaction prices are somewhat higher than the second-lowest cost.

second-price auction prices are similar, as the winning offer is competed down to the second-lowest cost.

Table 4 reports the results of a test supporting this "gap" explanation using an OLS regression of the difference between the average second-price auction price and the average verifiable negotiation price on the lowest cost, second-lowest cost, and regime dummy variable interactions. The price difference between the second-price auctions and the multilateral negotiations increases as the lowest cost decreases, holding the second-lowest cost constant. Similarly, the price difference between the second-price auctions and the multilateral negotiations increases as the second-lowest cost increases, holding the lowest cost constant.

The preceding results illustrate one reason to perform laboratory tests of theoretical predictions. If one considered verifiable multilateral negotiations to be like English auctions, then their predicted outcomes would be identical to the outcomes of second-price auctions. However, we find that the two institutions' outcomes differ when the sellers are responsible for making the initial offer, because the sellers' initial offers are less than the English auction's starting price, which is the buyer's value. This negotiating behavior may be explained by the sellers' rates of time preference, as they may be trying to hasten the negotiations by making aggressive initial offers.[15]

5. Across-Experiment Results

We designed this experiment to be comparable to the one reported in Thomas and Wilson [2001], which evaluates and compares behavior in first-price auctions and nonverifiable multilateral negotiations. That experiment was conducted in the same manner as the present one, with the following institutional differences. In the first-price auction, sequences of which are denoted by F, the seller offering the lowest price wins the auction and is paid the price it offered. In the nonverifiable multilateral negotiation, sequences of which are denoted by N, the sellers are not informed via the mechanism of the buyer's best current offer. Thus, whatever claims about competing offers the buyer makes in its communications with the sellers cannot be verified. We limit our across-experiment analysis to the first twelve periods (Regime 1), in which subjects have no prior experience with any of the four institutions, because the results of the earlier

---

[15] It also does not appear that this effect diminishes as the sellers gain experience.

experiment exhibited permanent institutional influences in later rounds that are not present here. We denote the expected price in institution k by P_k ($k = F, N, S, V$).

Finding 4: *In Regime 1, prices are weakly lowest in first-price auctions, followed in order by nonverifiable multilateral negotiations, verifiable multilateral negotiations, and second-price auctions. With two sellers, the ranking of transaction prices is $P_F < P_N = P_V < P_S$. With four sellers, the ranking of transaction prices is $P_F = P_N < P_V < P_S$.*

Evidence: Table 5 reports the results of a linear mixed-effects analysis that combines the 16 sessions in Thomas and Wilson [2001] with the 16 reported here, with the transaction price as the dependent variable. The two fixed effects that are not self-explanatory are defined as follows: *Negotiation* equals 1 for nonverifiable and verifiable multilateral negotiation sessions and equals 0 otherwise, and *Verifiable* equals 1 for verifiable multilateral negotiation sessions and equals 0 otherwise. Thomas and Wilson [2001] find that $P_F = P_N$ with four sellers, and that $P_F < P_N$ with two sellers.[16] In Finding 2 above we find that $P_V < P_S$ with both two and four sellers. That $P_N < P_V$ with four sellers is captured by the *Verifiable* fixed effect, which measures how much four-seller verifiable multilateral negotiation prices differ from four-seller nonverifiable multilateral negotiation prices. We find that four-seller verifiable multilateral negotiation prices exceed four-seller nonverifiable multilateral negotiation prices by $\hat{\beta}_3 = 0.613$, which is significant (*p*-value = 0.0345). For the two-seller treatment, the sum of the *Verifiable* and *Two* × *Verifiable* coefficients captures how much two-seller verifiable multilateral negotiations differ from two-seller nonverifiable multilateral negotiations. We find that $\hat{\beta}_3 + \hat{\beta}_6 = -0.29$, which is insignificant at conventional confidence levels (*p*-value = 0.2555). ∎

The most interesting aspect of Finding 4 is that credible verification of offers has no effect on prices in multilateral negotiations with two sellers, but it increases prices with four sellers. One way to understand this result is to consider the first-price auction and second-price auction as baseline polar cases. Behavior in the first-price auction reflects sellers' concern and lack of information about their rivals' price-setting behavior. In contrast, behavior in the second-price auction reflects sellers' lack of concern about their rivals' price-setting, which follows from the existence of a dominant strategy. In the verifiable multilateral negotiations, sellers are well informed about their rivals' price-setting and consequently set higher prices than in the first-price auctions. In the nonverifiable multilateral negotiations, the sellers' lack of concrete information about their rivals potentially influences behavior.

In the four-seller nonverifiable multilateral negotiation, having three rivals taking hidden actions is sufficient to induce behavior as aggressive as in the corresponding first-price auction. However, in the two-seller setting, having only a single rival acting secretly does not induce such aggressive behavior. In Thomas and Wilson [2001], we find that the divergence in outcomes of the first-price auction and nonverifiable multilateral negotiation with two sellers is driven by occasions in which there is a large gap between the lowest and second-lowest cost. It appears that in negotiations with two sellers, a seller with low costs is sufficiently confident about the likelihood its rival has high costs that the additional information available in the verifiable multilateral negotiations has relatively little value. Hence, the prices are the same in both negotiation formats. In contrast, the additional information increases the sellers' prices and profits when there are four sellers.

6. Conclusion

In this paper we use the experimental method to examine how the verifiability of offers affects both the outcomes of multilateral negotiations, and the relationship between the outcomes of multilateral negotiations and of different auction formats. At the within-experiment level, with both two and four sellers we find that transaction prices are statistically lower in verifiable multilateral negotiations than in second-price auctions, but that the institutions are equally efficient. Sellers in the second-price auctions largely follow their unique dominant strategy, so the market price is approximately equal to the second-lowest cost. Prices are lower in the verifiable multilateral negotiations, because in some instances the low-cost seller's initial offer is below its next-closest rival's cost, which eliminates the need for further negotiation. This unanticipated behavior contradicts in part our hypothesis that the two institutions would have identical outcomes.

At the across-experiment level, with both two and four sellers we find a consistent ranking of transaction prices across the four institutions. Prices are always lowest in first-price auctions, followed in turn by nonverifiable negotiations, verifiable negotiations, and second-

---

[16] This is reaffirmed in Table 5 with $\hat{\beta}_2 = -0.00$ (p-value = 0.9974) and $\hat{\beta}_5 = 0.79$ (p-value = 0.0521), respectively.

price auctions. Second-price auction prices always strictly exceed the other prices. With two sellers, nonverifiable and verifiable negotiation prices are statistically indistinguishable, while with four sellers, first-price auction and nonverifiable negotiation prices are statistically indistinguishable.

In addition to providing evidence about behavior in multilateral negotiations, our results have implications for institutional design. First, we find that providing sellers with more information about their rivals' price-setting behavior surprisingly leads to higher rather than lower prices in multilateral negotiations. Moreover, this difference would be even larger if the verifiable multilateral negotiations began with nonserious offers at the buyer's value, as then the prices in the verifiable negotiations would be even higher. This price ranking is reminiscent of the price ranking of second-price and first-price auctions. One could argue that in both first-price auctions and nonverifiable multilateral negotiations, similar factors contribute to the sellers' being more aggressive in their price-setting behavior, relative to the dominance-solvable second-price auctions and to the more informationally rich verifiable multilateral negotiations.

Second, we find that buyers in our setting should prefer to employ first-price auctions rather than either type of multilateral negotiation, assuming that multilateral negotiations are more costly than auctions in terms of the time spent determining the transaction price. As the latter assumption appears reasonable, this conclusion raises the question of why first-price auctions are not observed more frequently in common transactions. One explanation is that reputation effects create a barrier for buyers trying to implement first-price auctions. For example, a car buyer is a short-run player in the market for new automobiles, and hence is unlikely to be concerned about maintaining a reputation. If the car buyer approaches several dealers and tells them that he wants their best offer, as in a first-price auction, then the sellers would be foolish to actually submit their first-price offers. If the buyer thought he had received first-price offers, then he still would want to haggle with the dealers. Moreover, the dealers might be willing to make concessions if asked, because each knows that if he currently has the second-lowest offer, then he may yet get a profitable sale by reducing his price. Thus, the buyer's inability to commit to the procurement format likely inhibits his use of what appears to be the preferred institution. In our experiment, the buyer was exogenously committed to this format, which provided a constraint on his behavior that likely does not generally exist in actual transactions.

The implications of our results and inferences about their generality are limited by the scope of our experiment and would benefit from further research. First, it would be useful to extend our analysis to settings with different numbers of sellers or with asymmetries across sellers. Second, it would be interesting to let the buyer select his preferred institution, or be unable to commit not to haggle upon receiving the sellers' initial offers. Third, if participation is costly, then any comparison of institutions must consider the sellers' incentives to participate.

References

Cason, T. (1995). "An Experimental Investigation of the Seller Incentives in the EPA's Emission Trading Auction," *American Economic Review* 85, 905-922.

Chamberlin, E., (1948). "An Experimental Imperfect Market," *Journal of Political Economy* 56, 95-108.

Coppinger, V., Smith, V., and Titus, J. (1980). "Incentives and Behavior in English, Dutch, and Sealed-Bid Auctions," *Economic Inquiry* 43, 1-22.

Cox, J., Roberson, B., and Smith, V. (1982). "Theory and Behavior of Single Object Auctions," Vol. 2, Research in Experimental Economics, General Editor, V. Smith, (Greenwich: JAI, Press).

Cox, J., Smith, V., and Walker, J. (1983). "A Test That Discriminates between Two Models of the Dutch-First Auction Non-Isomorphism," *Journal of Economic Behavior and Organization* 4, 205-219.

Cox, J., Smith, V., and Walker, J. (1988). "Theory and Individual Behavior of First-Price Auctions," *Journal of Risk and Uncertainty* 1(1), 61-99.

Holt, C. (1980). "Competitive Bidding for Contracts Under Alternative Auction Procedures," *Journal of Political Economy* 88(3), 433-445.

Kagel, J., Harstad, R., and Levin, D. (1987). "Information Impact and Allocation Rules in Auctions with Affiliated Private Values," *Econometrica* 55, 1275-1304.

Laird, N. M., and Ware, J. H. (1982). "Random-Effects Models for Longitudinal Data," *Biometrics* 38, 963-974.

Longford, N. T. (1993). Random Coefficient Models. (New York: Oxford University Press).

McAfee, R.P., and McMillan, J. (1987). "Auctions and Bidding," *Journal of Economic Literature* 25, 699-738.

McAfee, R.P., and McMillan, J. (1996). "Analyzing the Airwaves Auction," *Journal of Economic Perspectives* 10, 159-175.

Milgrom, P., and Weber, R. (1982). "A Theory of Auctions and Competitive Bidding," *Econometrica* 50, 1089-1122.

Roth, A., and Ockenfels, A. (2001). "Last-Minute Bidding and the Rules for Ending Second-Price Auctions: Evidence from eBay and Amazon Auctions on the Internet," *American Economic Review*, forthcoming.

Smith, V. (1962). "An Experimental Study of Competitive Market Behavior," *Journal of Political Economy* 70 (2), 111-137.

Thomas, C.J., and Wilson, B.J. (2001). "A Comparison of Auctions and Multilateral Negotiations," *RAND Journal of Economics*, forthcoming.

Waehrer, K., and Perry, M. (1999). "The Effect of Mergers in Open Auction Markets." unpublished manuscript.

Wolfram, C. (1998). "Strategic Bidding in a Multiunit Auction: An Empirical Analysis of Bids to Supply Electricity in England and Wales," *RAND Journal of Economics* 29, 703-725.

Table 1. Average Transaction Price, Nash Predicted Second-Price Auction Price*, and Efficiency**

Sequence	*Two Sellers*			*Four Sellers*		
SSVS	Observed Price	Nash Prediction	Observed Efficiency	Observed Price	Nash Prediction	Observed Efficiency
Periods 1-12: *S*	4.17	3.62	98.1%	3.03	2.61	97.5%
Periods 13-28: *S*	4.49	4.26	98.7%	2.87	2.67	96.8%
Periods 29-40: *V*	2.53	3.90	93.8%	1.62	2.71	95.0%
Periods 41-46: *S*	4.89	4.63	99.3%	2.63	2.44	99.3%
VSSV						
Periods 1-12: *V*	3.46	3.62	96.9%	2.50	2.61	93.6%
Periods 13-28: *S*	4.69	4.26	97.9%	3.19	2.67	98.1%
Periods 29-40: *S*	4.03	3.90	97.6%	3.04	2.71	97.0%
Periods 41-46: *V*	3.35	4.63	95.6%	1.85	2.44	95.6%

*The Nash predicted second-price auction prices are conditional on the cost draws.
** Efficiency is defined to be $100\% \times (6 - \text{winner's cost})/(6 - \text{lowest cost draw})$.

Table 2. Estimates of the Linear Mixed-Effects Model for Price

$$Price_{ij} = \mu + e_i + \beta_1 Two_i + \beta_2 Verifiable_i + \beta_3 Two_i \times Verifiable_i + \varepsilon_{ij},$$

where $e_i \sim N(0, \sigma_1^2)$, $\varepsilon_{ij} \sim N(0, \sigma_{2,i}^2)$.

	Estimate	Std. Error	Degrees of Freedom*	t-statistic	p-value
Regime 1: Periods 1 – 12					
μ	3.080	0.179	176	17.251	0.0000
Two	1.133	0.299	12	3.787	0.0013†
Verifiable	-0.590	0.257	12	-2.300	0.0402
Two × Verifiable	-0.119	0.389	12	-0.305	0.7652
			192 Obs.		
			$H_a: \beta_2 + \beta_3 \neq 0$		0.0319
Regime 2: Periods 13 – 28					
μ	2.886	0.168	240	17.159	0.0000
Two	1.608	0.238	12	6.747	0.0000†
Verifiable History	0.409	0.221	12	1.845	0.0898
Two × Verifiable History	-0.119	0.310	12	-0.386	0.7066
			256 Obs.		
			$H_a: \beta_2 + \beta_3 \neq 0$		0.2069
Regime 3: Periods 29 – 40					
μ	3.210	0.245	174	13.085	0.0000
Two	0.824	0.354	12	2.330	0.0191†
Verifiable	-1.621	0.342	12	-4.734	0.0005
Two × Verifiable	0.060	0.515	12	0.116	0.9095
			190‡ Obs.		
			$H_a: \beta_2 + \beta_3 \neq 0$		0.0016
Regime 4: Periods 41 – 46					
μ	2.669	0.240	80	11.144	0.0000
Two	2.258	0.364	12	6.200	0.0000†
Verifiable	-0.726	0.342	12	-2.125	0.0276†
Two × Verifiable	-0.671	0.498	12	-1.348	0.2025
			96 Obs.		
			$H_a: \beta_2 + \beta_3 < 0$		0.0012†

*N.B. The linear mixed effects model for repeated measures treats each session as one degree of freedom with respect to the treatments. Hence, with four parameters, there are 12 degrees of freedom for the estimates of the treatment fixed effects (16 sessions – 4 parameters).
†One-sided test.
‡There were two cases in which the buyer did not accept any offer, both in the two-seller treatment when both sellers' costs were relatively high.
Note: The linear mixed-effects model is fit by maximum likelihood. For brevity, the session random effects are not included in this table or any others.

Table 3. Estimates of the Linear Mixed-Effects Model for Efficiency

$$Efficiency_{ij} = \mu + e_i + \gamma_1 Two_i + \gamma_2 Verifiable_i + \gamma_3 Two_i \times Verifiable_i + \varepsilon_{ij},$$

where $e_i \sim N(0, \sigma_1^2)$, $\varepsilon_{ij} \sim N(0, \sigma_2^2)$.

	Estimate	Std. Error	Degrees of Freedom*	t-statistic	p-value
Regime 1: Periods 1 – 12					
μ	97.51	1.43	176	68.05	0.0000
Two	0.61	2.03	12	0.30	0.7697
Verifiable	-3.93	2.03	12	-1.94	0.0764
Two × Verifiable	2.67	2.87	12	0.93	0.3702
			192 Obs.		
				H_a: $\gamma_2 + \gamma_3 \neq 0$	0.5456
Regime 2: Periods 13 – 28					
μ	96.75	1.40	240	68.88	0.0000
Two	1.94	1.99	12	0.98	0.3479
Verifiable History	1.34	1.99	12	0.67	0.5133
Two × Verifiable History	-2.17	2.81	12	-0.77	0.4539
			256 Obs.		
				H_a: $\gamma_2 + \gamma_3 \neq 0$	0.6812
Regime 3: Periods 29 – 40					
μ	97.02	2.11	176	45.90	0.0000
Two	0.60	2.99	12	0.20	0.8432
Verifiable	-2.00	2.99	12	-0.67	0.5170
Two × Verifiable	-1.81	4.23	12	-0.43	0.6764
			192 Obs.		
				H_a: $\gamma_2 + \gamma_3 \neq 0$	0.2273
Regime 4: Periods 41 – 46					
μ	99.25	2.34	80	42.47	0.0000
Two	0.02	3.31	12	0.01	0.9950
Verifiable	-3.64	3.31	12	-1.10	0.2923
Two × Verifiable	-1.69	4.67	12	-0.36	0.7236
			96 Obs.		
				H_a: $\gamma_2 + \gamma_3 \neq 0$	0.1326

Table 4. OLS Regression of the Difference of Average Second-Price Auction and Average Verifiable Negotiation Prices

Variable*	Estimate	Std. Error	t-statistic	p-value
Intercept	-0.21	0.17	-1.22	0.2279
Lowest Cost	-0.34	0.13	-2.69	0.0096
Second-Lowest Cost	0.48	0.09	5.20	0.0000
Lowest Cost × *Regime 3*	-0.38	0.15	-2.47	0.0166
Second-Lowest Cost × *Regime 3*	0.37	0.10	3.69	0.0005
Lowest Cost × *Regime 4*	-0.13	0.21	-0.64	0.5217
Second-Lowest Cost × *Regime 4*	0.09	0.12	0.77	0.4470

Adj. R^2 = 68.7%

Obs.= 60 = 30 periods × 2 (*Two* vs. *Four*)

*An $F_{7,46}$-test for 7 other variables including the dummy variables *Two* and *Regimes 3* and *4*, and their interactions with *Lowest Cost* and *Second-Lowest Cost*, indicates that they are jointly insignificant (p-value= 0.5036).

Table 5. Across-Experiment Estimates of the Linear Mixed-Effects Model for Price

$$Price_{ij} = \mu + e_i + \beta_1 Two_i + \beta_2 Negotiation_i + \beta_3 Verifiable_i$$
$$+ \beta_4 2ndPriceAuction_i + \beta_5 Two_i \times Negotiation_i$$
$$+ \beta_6 Two_i \times Verifiable_i + \beta_7 Two_i \times 2ndPriceAuction_i + \varepsilon_{ij},$$

where $e_i \sim N(0, \sigma_1^2)$, $\varepsilon_{ij} \sim N(0, \sigma_{2,i}^2)$.

	Estimate	Std. Error	Degrees of Freedom	t-statistic	p-value
Regime 1: Periods 1 – 12					
μ	1.875	0.190	350	9.885	0.0000
Two	1.129	0.295	24	3.821	0.0004[†]
Negotiation	-0.001	0.266	24	-0.003	0.9974
Verifiable	0.613	0.274	24	2.242	0.0345
2ndPriceAuction	1.199	0.272	24	4.407	0.0002
Two × *Negotiation*	0.786	0.385	24	2.044	0.0521
Two × *Verifiable*	-0.898	0.367	24	-2.448	0.0220
Two × *2ndPriceAuction*	0.007	0.435	24	0.016	0.9871
				$H_a: \beta_3 + \beta_6 \neq 0$	0.2555
			382 Obs.		

[†]One-sided test.

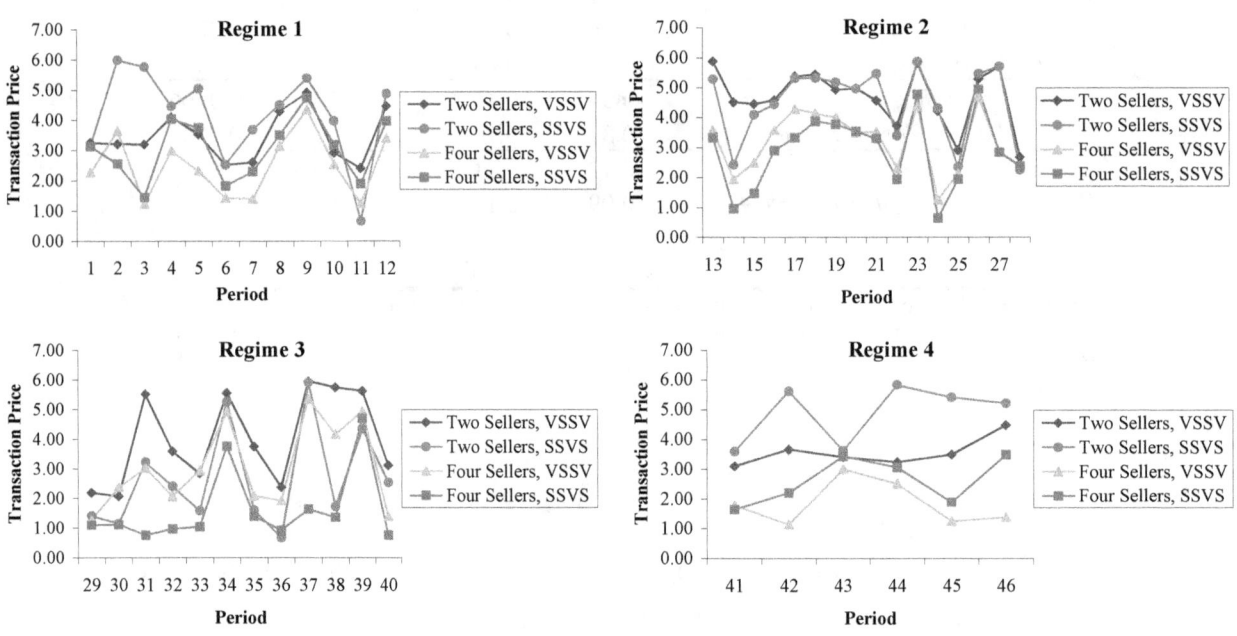

Figure 1. Average Transaction Prices By Regime

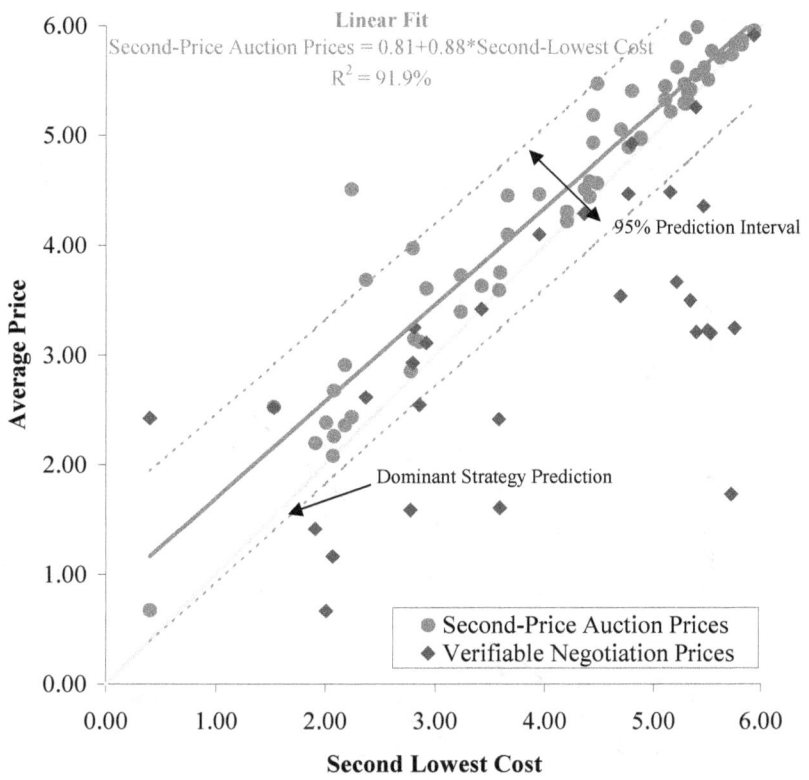

Panel (a) *Two-Seller* **Treatment**

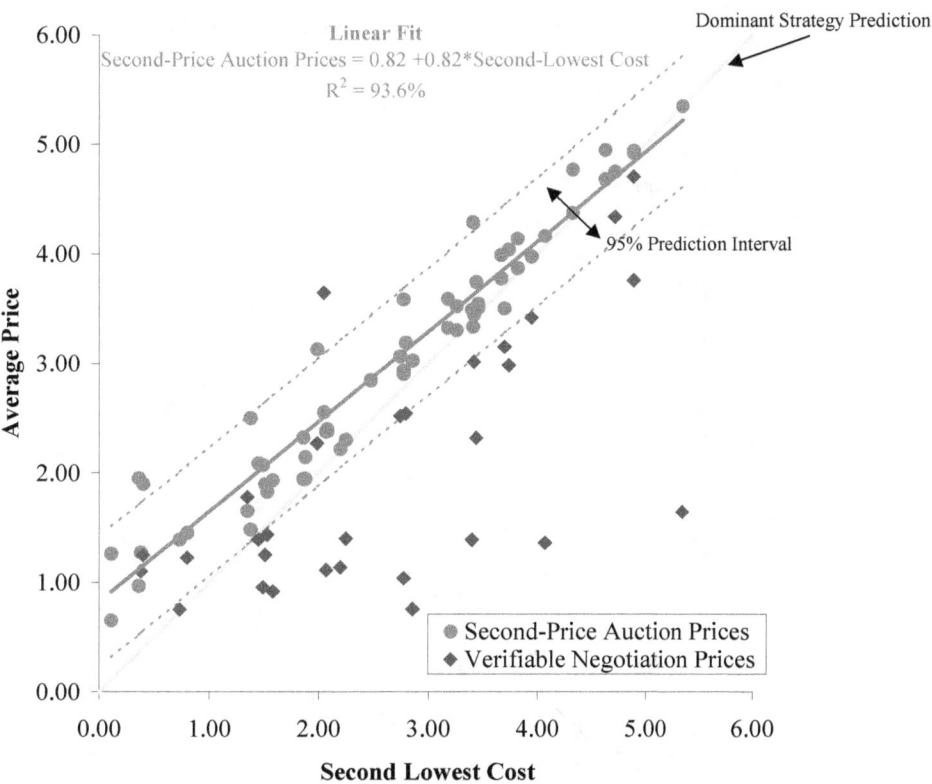

Panel (b) *Four-Seller* **Treatment**
Figure 2. Average Transaction Price versus Second-Lowest Cost

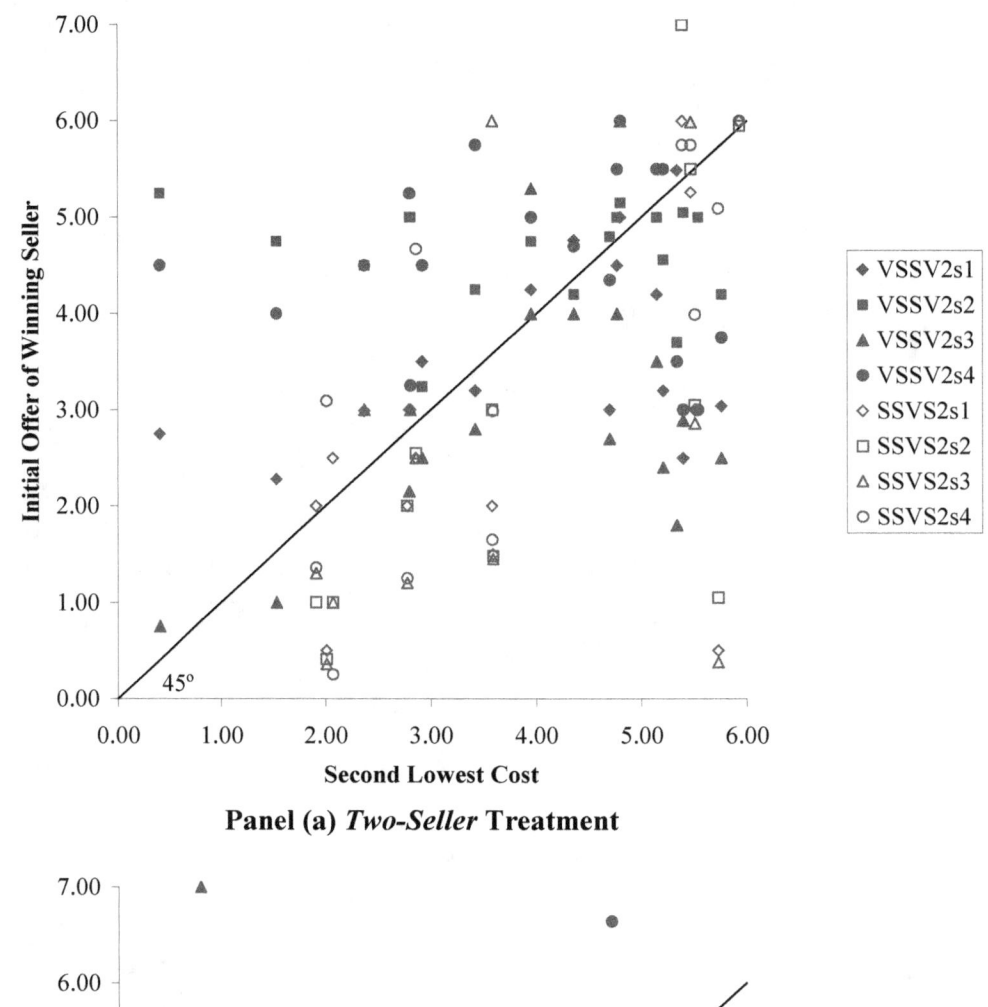

Panel (a) *Two-Seller* **Treatment**

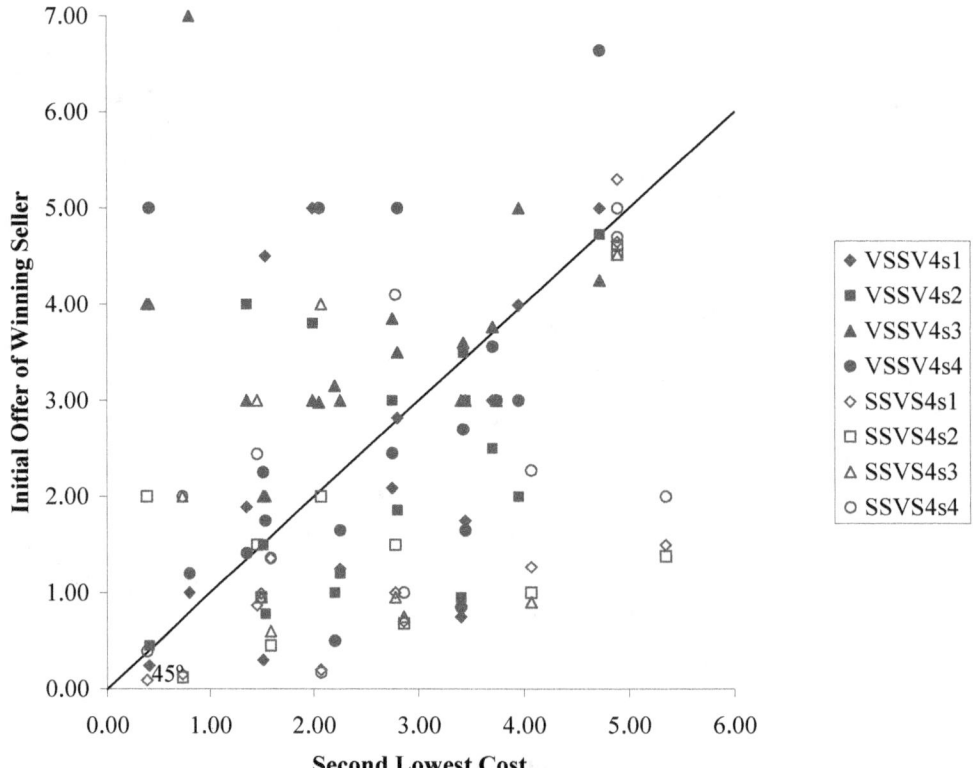

Panel (b) *Four-Seller* **Treatment**
Figure 3. Winning Seller's Initial Offer versus Second-Lowest Cost

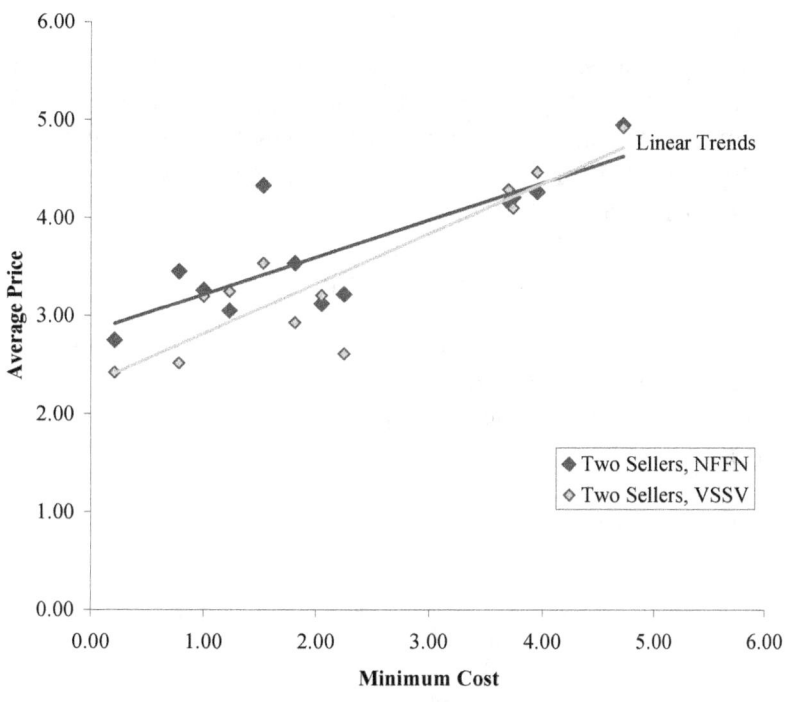

Panel (a) *Two-Seller* **Treatment**

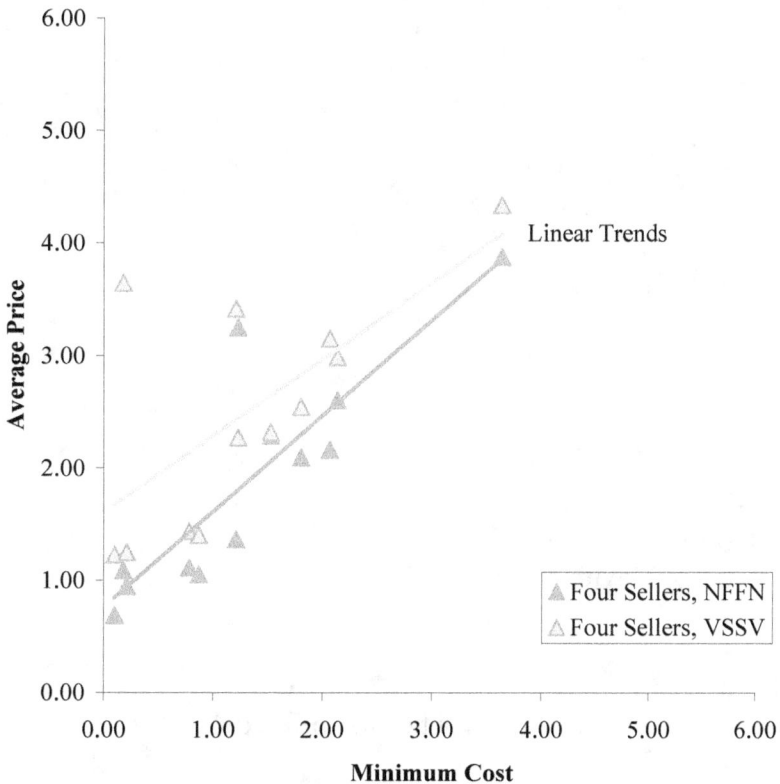

Panel (b) *Four-Seller* **Treatment**

Figure 4. Average Price versus Minimum Cost in Verifiable and Nonverifiable Multilateral Negotiations (Regime 1)

Appendix

The following selections are the written negotiations from the real-time ordered transcript and the descriptions of the offering activity. They illustrate that when the initial offer of the low-cost seller (o_1) is greater than the second-lowest cost ($c_{(2)}$) the final price is equal to the second-lowest cost. However, when the initial offer for the low-cost seller is less than the second-lowest cost, the final price is the initial offer of the low-cost seller.

Examples when $o_1 > c_{(2)}$

Four Seller *VSSV*, Session 2
Seller 3's initial offer was 2.50 with a cost of 0.80.
Seller 4's initial offer was 10.00 with a cost of 0.10.
Seller 1's cost was 1.00.
Seller 2's cost was 5.54.
Final price is 0.80, paid to Seller 4.

PERIOD 3
[Seller 1]: I split the profit 50/50.
[Buyer to Seller 1]: 3 in l\the lead
[Buyer to Seller 2]: 3 still has it
[Seller 1]: How about this?
[Buyer to Seller 4]: come on man, you gotta be kidding me
[Seller 2]: 2.50 -- why?
[Seller 2]: why so low?
[Buyer to Seller 1]: Good, your almost there
[Buyer to Seller 2]: Don't know, I'm just the buyer
[Seller 2]: loosing profit...
[Buyer to Seller 3]: you want it?
[Seller 3]: yeh
[Buyer to Seller 2]: Going for broke?
[Buyer to Seller 4]: Wow
[Seller 1]: Man! I can't go for least than it
[Seller 1]:
[Seller 2]: common...this is a joke....
[Buyer to Seller 2]: I know, I have to watch out for my interests though
[Seller 2]: .60???
[Buyer to Seller 4]: Alright, its yours

Two Seller *VSSV*, Session 2
Seller 1's initial offer was 4.80 with a cost of 1.53.
Seller 2's initial offer was 5.50 with a cost of 4.70.
Seller 2 drops price to 4.79.
Seller 1 responds with 4.70.
Seller 2 matches 4.70 (at cost).
Final price is 4.70 (buyer buys from Seller 1 who first offered 4.70).

PERIOD 5
[Buyer to Seller 2]: no way
[Buyer to Seller 2]: keep going or no business
[Seller 2]: gotta cover my costs here

Examples when $o_1 < c_{(2)}$

Four Seller *SSVS*, Session 3
Seller 1's initial offer was 0.90 with a cost of 0.37.
Seller 3 had the second-lowest cost at 4.07.
Seller 2's cost was 5.73.
Seller 4's cost was 4.11.
Final price is 0.90.

PERIOD 38
[Seller 2]: how do you like the product
[Seller 3]: i lose
[Buyer to Seller 1]: i think this time u really need money
[Buyer to Seller 2]: i hate it man..too much
[Seller 2]: well what's the price that u want it at
[Buyer to Seller 3]: y u will see 4.20 the highest
[Buyer to Seller 2]: seller 1 is selling at .85
[Seller 1]: i think you're the one who wants the money :)
[Seller 2]: aites..go for it then!
[Buyer to Seller 1]: thaz y ur charging high
[Seller 3]: just buy it at the .90 offer you have
[Buyer to Seller 3]: its .80
[Seller 3]: no it isnt i can see the lowes submitted ask
[Buyer to Seller 1]: man u will surely lose..i will buy froom u if ur price comes 15 cents ..down
[Seller 1]: how about five cents
[Buyer to Seller 1]: 10 cents..do it no time..or bye
[Seller 1]: seven cents
[Buyer to Seller 1]: okay
[Seller 3]: its stilll .90

Two Seller *VSSV*, Session 1
Seller 1's initial offer was 3.00 with a cost of 1.53.
Seller 2's initial offer was 5.00 with a cost of 4.70.
Final price is 3.00.

PERIOD 5

No written negotiation. Seller 2 cannot compete with an offer of 3.00 and so the buyer accepts Seller 1's initial offer.

Four Seller *VSSV*, Session 2
Seller 1's initial offer was 4.00 for a cost of 3.95.
Seller 2's initial offer was 4.82 for a cost of 4.77.
Seller 3's initial offer was 6.00 for a cost of 5.98.
Seller 4's initial offer was 2.00 for a cost of 1.21.
Final price is 2.00.

PERIOD 12

No written negotiation. Sellers 1,2, and 3 cannot compete with an offer of 2.00 and so the buyer accepts Seller 4's initial offer.

www.ingramcontent.com/pod-product-compliance
Lightning Source LLC
Chambersburg PA
CBHW081821170526
45167CB00008B/3486